Modern Wedding Poems
by
Ms Moem

Table Of Contents

I Choose You

Life can be thought as a series of choices made;
We hope to look back and smile as our memories are replayed.
Those once in a lifetime moments aren't always quick to show
But when they do materialise, then somehow you just know.

I am happier now than I ever thought I would be;
I love the person you are and the person you make me.
We share an understanding, we share hopes and goals
Together, united, we're two halves of one whole.

I will never take for granted that you've given me your heart
And I gently carry it with me whenever we are apart.
In return, I give you mine, to cherish and to hold.
No promise is too great to make, you're worth your weight in gold.

Promises made. Vows declared.
A dream to build. A life to share.
I'm proud to utter the words 'I do'
As it tells the world that I choose you.

Vows

Today I pledge to spend my life, with you, day in, day out
And from the rooftops words of love I proudly stand and shout.
I promise you will always have my trusty hand to hold
With feelings of togetherness that never will grow old.
Our marriage, like a work of art, we'll craft in collaboration
With each new day another win, a cause for celebration.
I undertake the happy task of always taking care
To show you that I love you and when you need me, I'll be there.
As we build our future we shall do what suits us both.
These rings exchanged with love serve as tokens of our troth.
Trust me when I tell you that you mean the world to me
And we can share our days and nights, as long as you agree
To be the one to hold my hand when choppy waters swell;
Our love story a unique tale, that only we can tell.
As we say our wedding vows, you have my word, my bond
That I'll be sure to love you, and only you, my whole life long.

Twas The Night Before The Wedding

Twas the night before the wedding, and in a young bride's dreams
Ran thoughts of blissful lifelong love, and everything that means.
Thoughts of morning waking, beside the one she loved;
Fitting together perfectly, like hand fits to a glove.

Twas the night before the wedding & a young groom's sleepy smile
Re-lived the story of the girl, who captured his heart with style.
The moment that he saw her, he knew it was for life
And he knew he'd found the lady who was destined to be his Wife.

Twas the night before the wedding, and guests from far and wide
Looked forward to the occasion of witnessing this marriage,
with pride.
Their best clothes pressed and ready, and gifts prepared to give
Ready to help create memories, to be cherished as long as we live.

On the morning of the wedding, all parties gathered together
To celebrate this union, that is bound in love, forever.
And everyone there present, was overjoyed to see
The Bride and Groom united and as happy as happy can be.

Forever

Will you love me when I'm ancient
Will you feel the same as today?
Will I still make you have butterflies
And feel proud in every way.

Will you still chat to me daily
And try to make me laugh?
Will you still give me a cuddle
And sneak a peek at me in the bath?

Will you still wake up each morning
And turn to me with a grin?
Will you still tell me I'm beautiful
And mean, outside and in.

Will you always want to hold me
And want me to feel blissfully safe?
Will you still know what I am thinking
Just by reading what lies on my face.

And if you still want to go ahead with this
Then here's to our life together
So answer yes to all these questions
Then there's no doubt this will last forever.

I Am Yours For All Of Time

You are mine for all of time
And I am yours.
I call for love, for care sublime,
You come, no pause.
When you need me, right there I'll be
I hear your call.
Your confidante, my heart responds,
I give my all.

To one from two, we say "We do"
Now marriage bonds.
We carve our space, we found the place
Our hearts belong.
Worlds rearranged and vows exchanged
We stand together.
One and the same, we share a name;
Love grows forever.

With those who care, this day we share;
Our joy enhanced.
A family affair, a happy pair
A love advanced.
One life to live, much love to give
Our paths align.
It's you I adore, I'm eternally yours
For all of time.

Who Knew

Who knew that this would happen
Who knew that this would be
Who knew that love would blossom and excel for you & me.

Who knew you'd drive me crazy
Who knew you'd be the one
Who knew you'd be the lifeblood that makes me go on & on.

Who knew it would be perfect
Who knew this match was true
Who knew that I would definitely be the only one for you.

Who knew it would propel us
Who knew that this was fate
In answer, I knew all of that, because you're my soulmate!

The One

You are the one!
But how did I know?
You make me feel wanted and make my heart glow.

You are the one!
You make me complete.
You're all I've ever wanted; so loving and sweet.

You are the one!
The other half of the story.
You tell me you love me and boldly adore me.

You are the one!
My undeniable other.
You are my best friend, my soulmate, my lover.

You are the one!
You are my life
You are my only & together we're husband and wife!

A Realistic Wedding Poem

Marriage is a journey, and not just a destination
That goes far beyond this wedding, this public celebration.
This is just the beginning of a path we'll travel together
With obstacles to overcome, and possible storms to weather.

One day we'll sit side by side, hands withered and bent
Thinking back over the years, the good times we have spent.
We'll remember the laughs. We'll recall special places
And look far beyond the greyed hair and softly lined faces.

So let's take it all in and cherish each day
No matter what happens, no matter what's thrown our way.
We're both realistic. Every day won't be a dream
But we're in this together, because we make a cracking team!

One Whole

There's a never-ending universe, that extends beyond the eye
And there are billions of people who lives simply pass us by.
But then there is the someone who,
whose life purpose has a goal
Of finding their perfect other half;
the one that makes them whole.

One soul made of patchwork, strands of our lives entwined.
One heart beating tirelessly, the rhythm of our lives defined.
One body standing confidently,
with boundless energy thriving
One life that is made for living,
and not just simply surviving.

How Do I Love You

How do I love you?
You're the one I love the most.
You're the sugar to my coffee.
You're the butter to my toast.

How do I know you?
You're the one who's got my back.
You're the light that guides me home each night.
You are the beacon on my life's map.

How do I feel you?
You're the blood in my veins.
You're the surge of daily butterflies.
I'm the circuit. You're the mains.

How do I show you?
You're the twinkle in my eye.
You're the bitten lip in my smile.
You're the happiest tears I cry.

So how do I love you?
With heart gladly given.
With moonlit serenity,
The sun, it is risen.

I Love You Because

I love you because you're thoughtful.
I love you because you're nice.
I love you because you catch spiders
And I don't have to ask you twice.

I love you because you're wonderful.
I love you because you're fun.
I love you because you listen
And we share all the things we have done.

I love you because you're faithful.
I love you because you're sweet.
I love you because you give me a hug
When I feel I am dead on my feet.

I love you because you're gentle.
I love you because you care.
I love you because you are sensitive
And I know that you'll always be there.

I love you because you are awesome.
I love all the things that you do.
I love you because you are one for me.
I love you because you are you.

Let There Be Love

Let the bells chime
And confetti be thrown
As we celebrate a love
That has blossomed and grown.

Let there be suits
And dresses of satin
As cards of congratulations
Hit your welcome home matting.

Let there be family
And lots of close friends
As a groom declares his love
Will never have an end.

Let there be speeches
And a loving first dance
With tales of true love
Told in a bride's glance.

Let there be music
And smiles and laughter
As we all come together
To wish you a happy ever after.

A Love Story

Boy meets girl the story goes;
She gives his heart a lift.
Captivated by her charms
He showers her with gifts.
The first day he gives her a rose.
She blushes baby pink.
Those little crinkles round her nose
Take him to the brink.
The next day he brings her a box,
A necklace held within.
Her eyes light up and then he spots
Her dimples when she grins.
Another day, another gift,
Another chance to shine.
He takes her for a lovely meal
And buys her vintage wine.
The days roll by, the gifts pour in,
The boy is struck by fear.
It's certain that the day will come
He'll run out of ideas.
And lo, that day did happen.
He approached their date with dread.
She laid her hand upon his arm
And very simply said.....
Before you spend a penny more
I think that you should know.
It's not the things you buy for me.
You had me at hello.

Tell Me

Tell me all your secrets
Tell me all your dreams
Tell me where you came from
And all the things you've seen.

Tell me all the little things
That rattle round your head.
Tell me how you really feel;
Don't let things go unsaid.

You can tell me when you're happy
You can tell me when you're sad
You can tell me when I wind you up
That I really make you mad.

Tell me that tomorrow
Will always be a brand new day.
Tell me that together
We will always be okay.

Then tell me that you love me
Tell me that you care
Tell me there's nowhere you'd rather be.
Tell me you'll always be there.

I Promise

I promise I'll be there for you, with each beat of my heart.
I promise I'll be there for you, in times both bright and dark.
I promise I'll be there for you when you just want to talk.
I promise I'll be there for you, by your side as we walk.
I promise I'll be there for you, no matter where we are,
I promise I'll be there for you, I swear it on the stars.
I promise I'll be there for you, I promise I am sure;
I promise that I love you and I shall forever more!

Thank you for reading
and if you use
any of these poems at your wedding,
please drop me a line and let me know!

Ms Moem xx

Printed in Great Britain
by Amazon